Bad Summon

THE AGHA SHAHID ALI PRIZE IN POETRY

Bad Summon

Philip Schaefer

Foreword by David Baker

THE UNIVERSITY OF UTAH PRESS
Salt Lake City

AGHA SHAHID ALI

PRIZE IN POETRY

The Agha Shahid Ali Prize in Poetry
Series Editor: Katharine Coles
Advisory Editor: Paisley Rekdal

The Defiance House Man colophon is a registered trademark of
The University of Utah Press. It is based on a four-foot-tall Ancient
Puebloan pictograph (late PIII) near Glen Canyon, Utah.

Library of Congress Cataloging-in-Publication Data

Names: Schaefer, Philip, author.
Title: Bad summon / Philip Schaefer.
Description: Salt Lake City : The University of Utah Press, [2017]
    Series: Agha Shahid Ali prize in poetry | Some of these poems
    first appeared in other publications, sometimes in other forms. |
    Contents notes from ECIP table of contents. |
Identifiers: LCCN 2017021789 (print) | LCCN 2017025290 (ebook)
    ISBN 9781607815549 () | ISBN 9781607815549
    ISBN 9781607815549q(pbk.)
Subjects: | LCGFT: Poetry.
Classification: LCC PS3619.C31275 (ebook) | LCC PS3619.C31275
    A6 2017 (print) | DDC 811/.6--dc23
LC record available at https://lccn.loc.gov/2017021789

Printed and bound in the United States of America.

For Natalie

Contents

III. HELL FEELINGS

Foreword
David Baker

Bad things have happened. Hearts have been broken. People have been hurt and in turn they hurt. There are rips and tears all along the social fabric—so much so that it's hard to see beyond a moment or feel any measure of certainty—and nature, the green world, our home, has been assailed and degraded. Philip Schaefer writes from the edges of these and other disasters and makes his uneasy poems in the active aftermath. It's messy here, vexed and ever-shifting, and Schaefer's blend of intensity and offhandedness creates an equally uncomfortable residence for his work, as in "[In this one I'm wearing a paper bag]," where the title swings into the poem's first line:

> over my head with cut-out eyes
> and a slit for the horse of my tongue.
> I walk around town letting children
> and transients draw their names
> on my face. Each signature stitched
> like a scar.

Bad Summon is a vivid, soulful new book of poems, a first book by a young poet with serious talent, a lean style, and a beguiling, slightly off-kilter voice. Even the grammatical slippage of the book's title suggests some of Schaefer's tactic—akimbo, disrupted, repaired but not fixed. "I've written a declaration of independence / on the bathroom mirror," he says among the residue of a broken or gone-wrong relationship. About marriage, but also about the slow-burning paradox of the private life, erotic and ashamed at once, he writes, "We haven't made love in weeks / but goddamn do we hold hands in public / to hide it." Schaefer's voice projects an offhandedness, at least at first, an ah-shucks bruised quality; but that belies the subtle, precise care and intricacy of the poet's craft and measure of skill.

There are echoes of forebears throughout the fifty-five poems of *Bad Summon*. Richard Hugo, that great Missoula presence, is clearly one of those echoes, both for a slightly wrecked tone and a formal constancy. "Say your life broke down" indeed. Likewise, for his solitary stance and stylistic clarity, Jack Gilbert. Like theirs, Schaefer's preferred form is a regular line—generally four or five beats—and an unencumbered stanza, plain and substantial as a four-square building:

> A cancerous goat walking around
> in fencepost circles is one way
> to describe this. You are dead.
> Everyone you loved is dead
> to you and a field of charred wheat
> flaking off the low Montana plains
> isn't enough to say we all beg
> for winter water. We contain
> multitudes. Miracles still fit
> into our pockets like watches,
> waltzes we've not yet stepped to.

Postromantic perhaps, Schaefer here in the opening lines of "Elegiac" also recalls Keats's "posthumous" projection of voice and Whitman's amplitude, turned stark, ironic, or at least diminished into a pocket-sized likeness of "miracles."

But if his form or troping recalls Hugo and Gilbert, Keats and Whitman, certainly his voice veers far away from their generally somber or sincere tones. For Schaefer, irony—dark humor—is a method of coping, and this strategy ranges for him from odd playfulness to an off-kilter complexity. In this way he's more akin to Mary Ruefle or Matthew Olzmann, yet his is an even darker humor than theirs. In the opening lines of "Barbiturate Talismania," Schaefer's strangeness both haunts and ironically enlivens an otherwise dulling life:

> This sadness, this halved skull
> filled with wildflowers. We arrive
> on a rickshaw of night clouds,
> winter air draped around us
> like a beached blue animal, wet
> and dry as milk. Cocoon gauze.
> What dies inside these chambers
> doesn't matter.

Schaefer uses irony as a solution to the merely mournful or plaintive. It offsets mere "sadness." Irony isn't a rare commodity in new poetry, to be sure. I appreciate that Schaefer rejects the easier intonations of sarcasm or the hipster's snarky jab, which infect the literary journals. His tone bears the inflection of a deeper existential plight or anxiety, a brooding gravity that might overpower any poem uttered with simple sincerity or equally simple sarcasm.

That's one of his secrets, I think. For every dark or perilous gesture, there's another motivation toward invention and newness. He's got a vivifying capability with image, as in "Once":

> I took a mason jar of fireflies
> and shook them
> like a snowglobe.
>
> So much death
> lighting up.
>
> Manhattan
> in my hands.

This little poem is haiku-like in its precision and image-making. If the shaken "snowglobe" of fireflies is both beautiful and brutal, then the next couplet is even more powerfully ironic, where death is nonetheless capable of providing light and energy. The surprising turn into the final stanza completes Schaefer's transfiguring microcosm: all of Manhattan in a mason jar.

This degree of constant surprise and of invention, these qualities of a new voice making original music, compel me more than anything else in Philip Schaefer's *Bad Summon*. It's a relatively interior sort of book, both intimate and isolate, and yet it is also fully connective. I *feel* more here than in many other new books of poems—more peril, heartbreak, catastrophe, sorrow, genuine soulfulness. Schaefer can speak in plural or collective ways, as well as in singular, in a kind of guarded autobiographical voice and then in a postapocalyptic one. But even more, it's this simple, powerful degree of surprise, of newness that I so much admire: "Grass makes sauce / of last fall's pumpkins." That's sheer poetry.

Philip Schaefer possesses a potent, distinct style—world-wise, more than a little battered, yet very alert. For all its world-woe, its fatigue and peril, *Bad Summon* is also vivid and oddly refreshing. For every "lone cannon" or shovelful of grief, Schaefer offers up his own brand of wry, transformative hope: "as if there were / a milk in this world / sweet enough to last." As if, indeed.

"Isn't this your life?"

—Richard Hugo

Suture

The moment we say alone we are
not. The sun tucks under the mouth
of a mountain yet still light fills
our skin. Every day a heart is pulled
out like a wet plum from one body
and placed inside another. Every day
someone comes home to a lover
packing her bags. It is normal
to fall asleep in pain and wake
with more. We break open
clouds by waiting long enough.
Behind this midnight other midnights
trace a face so familiar we touch
our cheekbones like twin moons.
With closed eyes we wonder what
we are to do with all this living.

I.

LUMINAL STATIC

The New World

Let's go back to when we were still undiscovered.
To when losing meant losing and we lost
everything. Our names, the candle of our bodies.
Small tokens of light clipping in and out
of us like bullet holes. Our skin a thing for fire.
Let's rub the moon between thumb and forefinger
until we disappear. There are galaxies of hurt
and in each of them we become masters.
We crawl up the throat of the sky like dying
animals and beg heaven to let us in. We don't
believe in anything worth saving. The fields
flashing in the quiet distance, the stars
raked from the chest of the night like glowing
leaves. In a way we are as still as the day
we were born. A pair of yellow eyes
floating in a tree, the idea of flight so close
we stretch back an arrow until we are the arrow.

The Unaccounted

Say we slept like effigies on a stranger's lawn.
      Sideways to the boats roping in, saltwater
            lapping the land so thick we could slick it
      through our hair. Say children surrounded us
with wooden knives and smoke bombs,
      their jeans as putrid as the corner ponds
            they were born in. Their teeth loose
      gravel, a new language for ruin or roll
over. Say a day before, a returned soldier
      drove into the woods and made out
            with his shotgun. Skull a split piñata,
      a fist of sun unraveling. For now let's say
the black lab in the truck isn't panting, stuck
      to leather, radio on. This isn't about us.
            Everyone in town is drinking brown fire
      to forget someone they read about
in the paper. Someone no one knew
      well enough. Here it is always almost
            summer. A beach of women probing their legs
      through water like herons. Teenagers staring,
pretending their eyes are tanning oil. Say we are
      old stone castles. That when the drawbridge drops
            the moat disappears like a name fingered on a window.

Evening News

A man shoots through
another man, his chest

a black sky of star holes.
On the trail a white male

plucks a girl's clothes off
like apples, articles and socks

found in the creek nearby.
The amber alert crawling

through our backyards.
We hold the bedspread

to our necks and pray
for less evidence, for

safe and endless water.
Fires plume the Bitterroot

en masse orange, twelve
hells combing the hillside.

A gas station clerk
found with his neck

boiled red in the register.
All for a night of light

heads. The football team
record resting on the arm

of a boy who is addicted
to the way he feels

after midnight, recently
acquitted. Some move

to be alone,
to be common

and replaceable
by mountainsides.

I hold on to myself
like a grenade.

Walk Slowly, Don't Stare

Actually, the problem is we're getting too bored
with hate. Children divorce their parents, parents
each other. Cows break down into leather or jerky
or what's the difference. Here's an American can.
Here's the mouth of the sky. Clouds foam back
like rolling heads. My new mantra: you must die
watching others die. Try saying it out loud
while you picture a face. Hold your hell feelings
high. Planes needle the horizon and the sun
starts bleeding all over again. This too is for you.
Nothing you love is waiting at the finish line.

Earthenware

A dying woman wraps cashmere around a dog who will never grow back its missing leg and in this way I want to open my chest to the morning. To brush blood orange nail polish along the toes of my sleeping wife, breathe in the alchemy on her mythic skin. The cairn along the abandoned railroad track leads to the sky and now I know moon more as direction than distance. Last night in Portland the street man shaved half a lung to tell us *you're a fucking liar*. I knew he meant me. His hair a flag I've never had to wave, his skin a music masked as massacre. If god then god save. If not then more free beer and autumn for all. The parking lot trees are on quiet fire and this must be enough reason to buy a banjo for someone I've never met. Is it so sick to knife my once-friend's name on the bar stall wall and carve an arrowed heart from the lone vowel? She doesn't remember she told me he was rough in bed — not so much a wooden horse but the memory of your father's voice before the bedroom door closes toward divorce. What makes me want to hold dead batteries in my hand I cannot say. Still I toss their weight high into the afternoon. Ask the sun to give back only what it can't. My head a pillow for electricity. A slant of ducks driving the air, diving for some pond to call home, though nothing is ever exactly what we want it to be.

Sisyphus Self

My wife is gorgeous. She throws bacon
fat into everything. The blanched greens,
the roux, her hair. If I could I would
rinse the hickory out with my tongue.
Instead I outline a coffin for myself
on the sidewalk, siphoning a bottle
of cheap feelings, smoking half a pack
of moonlight. I tell myself to stop
being so romantic. Tell myself to stay
good to the woman feathered in my bed.
On the curb I finger her shape against
a constellation of star bulbs. I breathe out
a line of ants. We haven't made love in weeks
but goddamn do we hold hands in public
to hide it. On the news tonight a newlywed
pushed her husband off a cliff in Glacier.
On the news I see myself pushing against
everywhere. Lately I fall over in fear.
I sleepwalk into the ground, letting spiders
cavern through my ears. There are ways
of letting things go: the mind, my wife,
our years. No one I know is dying.

Discipline

We're leaving our fantasies out in the open.
Our latticed legs, the chest whips.
We're on all fours like begging dogs.
Hello failure, hello my little french
whisperer. Immaculate milk streams down
the mirror, candied cherries float along
the hardwood river. This is a game of how long
can we stay together and say no to silence.
To wear a mouth mask with a red ball and suffer
the entire calendar of *as long as possible*.
We say threesome wholesome. We rinse
our hair in oil and breathe in the smoke.
We're discovering the new languages between
oh god and disaster. Old pictures loosening
from their frames. The walls rumbling
like california. Neighbors walk their ordinary
lives around in leashes, ears closed to the world
we've created, destroyed. Hate and thirst and cats
shivering beneath the moon where we stare off
past the night. The night as quiet as finishing.

Summer Blackout

We soaked towels in lighter fluid.
We lifted blood-lipped matches
to our faces, striking and smelling
everything that would burn between
our fingers. A line of ants climbing
up the gutter into a song of flame,
the box spring on the back porch,
whatever might become a mountain
of ash. We didn't want to be good
to each other. We fell on our lives
like bombs, tore our shirts into flags,
each country staked to the lawn,
the wind beating and us beating back.
We knew dogs with boot marks
branded into their sides. We knew
feral. Those years we called out war
to the forest just to see what might
appear within the trees. We held
the pins tight between our teeth,
grenades warm in our hands
like metallic dolls, dead birds
to kiss like the memory of flight.

Once

I took a mason jar of fireflies
and shook them
like a snowglobe.

So much death
lighting up.

Manhattan
in my hands.

Last week the world started destroying itself again. Images of a
girl without eyes, flat on a trampoline, the air around her more
gasoline than snow. God if god give us snow. A pewter we can
blow dust off, hold like pencils in the twitch of our fingers and
write new languages for freedom and distance. We await mercy
as if it's lost luggage. We draw faces of tropical fish against
airplane windows. God if god send rain. Endless pellets of
bluegrass and I'm sorry so sorry never again. A boy like a
yellow kite stuck in an apple tree, limbs vining into branches.
We cannot stand another flood. Will we forever be witness? We
interest the dark by standing long enough, orange tip of a
cigarette dying, glowing until the sun sucks up the throat of the
sky. We will not go inside. Most dogs never grow back their
missing legs. Some swans are never painted in pigments of
want. We try to give a name to everything we can't control. In
the middle of Montana, with backs broken by beauty, all we
know is cadaver, spleen, amethyst, smoke screen, grenade pins,
Christ's skin crinkling, newspaper ink, children laughing under
floorboards, deer stink, night sweats, beverages birthing forgive
forgot forever until we meet again. God if god if got if good
for nothing.

Overdose

They stapled his eyes open and saw nothing
but an empty beach. I wanted to dig my hands
deep through that sand, pull out two crescent moons
or a plastic gun. They said his heart was a dead car
battery. Each of their latex gloves blue as ambulance
sirens over his chest cavity. After a while they said
amphetamines. I can't remember who held the needle
but earlier at the house I watched him take metal to skin
as if pleasure were a hundred endangered doves
plumed in his veins. I saw neon suns explode
over an undiscovered ocean. There is a way
to love char as texture, to know you will never shower
the same again. They said or didn't say but I heard
that his brain activity was still crisp static, midnight
lights lining a pinball machine. That night I broke
my television like a bag of ice on the kitchen
floor and drove unfathomable swords into my own quiet
electricity. When they placed the unfamiliar tools
back on the clean rack, white towel still
white, they said nothing else. It sounded like sorry
or finally, a brass cartridge shell full with powder.

Barbiturate Talismania

This sadness, this halved skull
filled with wildflowers. We arrive
on a rickshaw of night clouds,
winter air draped around us
like a beached blue animal, wet
and dry as silk. Cocoon gauze.
What dies inside these chambers
doesn't matter. Some blood moons
implode and become a miracle
of tossed snow without body,
without obituary. We sew webs
in dark attic corners. Our chests
widen into lakes deep enough
for someone beautiful to drown in.
We let them. This is how desire
shapes like a map: we disappear.

I'm Keeping the Wooden Horse

The slit navel of my eye lights up the mirror and I hover for a split longer, pausing to whisper *what I own I barely know*. Metal comb, shower rod, lamb's hair. The trees crawl through the window after the wind licks them dry. On the other side, my wife dreams me running through an abandoned warehouse, head cupped in the *V* of my arms like a pigskin, directing my body from below. I am both Jaeger and prey. Dream logic and revolver. And isn't it true we are the first person we murder? Tonight I held her chin on my shoulder until she could drift and pull the trigger at me once again. How subverted this perversion, this other version we become. Lately we speak of moving to a country we cannot name. We stick pins in the map like star holes and let the cartography of our bodies decide between pleasure and snow and what's the difference. We were married in a bar, downing Molotovs, spitting out darts of fire. And that's where it ends until it begins. Penguins sliding until the water raptures them, swallowing the moon. A toothpick dog wandering off alone into death, filled with wild memory.

Practicing Invisible

I keep staring at this bent elbow of ducks
in the sky, wondering which of us will break
first. Eventually everything returns to glass.
My breath against a window, the ocean.
I cock back my finger to drop them
one by one into the town pond. I draw
a trophy for myself with the clouds.
If I could bring back the dead I would
only be able to bury them again.

Minor Dogma

I believe in snapping apples
from the hard joints of August.
I believe in holding them high
until they become the blood
marble eyes of hawks
over fields. I believe in the earth.
In the way rain fingers through it
like full moons of acid dropped
into a glass. I believe in taking nothing
back. I place my chest on the hardwood
floor and start to believe it's a small cut
of sun being cooled from behind
a distant galaxy. I feel the air
fold over me like a coffin lid. I believe
in Cambodia. In fishing through
ponds of rice paddies with silk
hands. The word *monsoon* beading
on my tongue until it forms a pool
where my teeth are the basements
of flooded buildings. Pull up the carpet,
pick out your ruined words. I peel
flies off the skin of dying fruit
and smear them on a napkin.
I flip it over and write: *if we are only*
clouds, picture me a wild animal.
Watch me foam over.

II.

[HIDEOUS] MIRACULOUS

[Yesterday I found myself awake]

in the shower with my shirt on,
searching for my breast bone
like a doorknob in a hallway
that doesn't exist. In this one
I am learning how to say *sponge*
without moving a muscle.
I contemplate what it means
to twitch. Contemplate which
Dakota I'd rather live in, having
never been. You told me
the Midwest was like two dogs
greeting each other. I don't understand
anything without distance. In this way
I am like you: greedy, not sorry.

Translating Poorly

You say things
like a plum

is breaking. Pipes
are dormant

fountains, so
let's move

to Kansas
City in a taxi.

You want me
to call out

the sky for
not responding

to your letter.
So what if

airplanes only
speak cursive.

What message
isn't better

left in a bottle.
Put it down.

You've been
relocking the car

doors for over
an hour.

You say things
like bougainvillea

are dreadful
creatures.

You curse Christ
in broken German.

I am not your liar.
I am not your liar.

[In this one we aren't exactly drowning]

but we are falling through water.
Quieter than we expect. Churning
is how we'll later describe it.
Our arms dig out two wet Cs,
a heart if you want to look at it
that way. Though the body is always
in between — that unoriginal arrow.

[In this one I'm wearing a paper bag]

over my head with cut-out eyes
and a slit for the horse of my tongue.
I walk around town letting children
and transients draw their names
on my face. Each signature stitched
like a scar. Each as foreign
as the day I was born. I'm trying to
become the animal you made of me.

[In this one you haven't left]

and the lilacs aren't devastating.
Fact: I'm being dramatic. A knife
undresses butter in my good hand
and I have that. I nibble on a biscuit,
tell myself I'm attractive, biting
the corners of my mouth
with the crumbles. Taste blood.

[A swarm of neighborhood dogs]

around the corner over a boy
on a bicycle. His legs electrical
fans, all cylinder and gear. I strike
and throw matches into a bucket
on the porch, the smell of science
going warm and black on my fingers.
I'm not mentioning you in this one.
I've written a declaration of independence
on the bathroom mirror. Your dark
crimson lipstick worn like graffiti
on my pants, my socks, which
I'm pulling up over my shins
like excess skin. Sometimes
it's necessary for one people
to dissolve. Sometimes
we shed our names.

I've been dipping my finger in this happy hour martini for half
a week now. My mouth is a ballroom. My tongue a wedding
dress floating up from the basement of a pond. Like romance I
don't shut up. I eat olive after olive. After all this there's
nothing but The King and number one-thirty-three on this
neon lit machine. Wise men don't say what wise men don't say.
But mostly it's true: I miss your clouds, your bubblegum yawn.
Barkeep keeps calling me Joe and I can't help but look over my
shoulder. Outside the moon drools out astronauts. What we
used to call stars falling. What we used to call anything floating
with root beer. On the train today a man sang into his necktie.
Tapped it twice for reverb. He wore a human face the shape of
Indiana. When you're old, imagine us in violet: I grease back
my genius hair and step on stage. I dip the mic and make a
spark through its metal, buzzing lips. Listen, my voice is
drumming. Cup your ear.

[In this one the car still runs]

and we drive to the basin, peel off
our clothes like exorcised ghosts.
We get biblical under the hot choke
of sun. Our bodies amplify — waves
lapping waves. We towel off with nothing.

[In this one you are taking the creek]

to your mouth, through your hair.
You want to rinse yourself
of last night's fire and I should
have known this would become
a foreshadowing moment.
We spent the night with the night
as if the stars were still neon
stickers glued to the bedroom
ceiling. The wind did something
through the sleeping bag and I felt
the smooth jazz of your left thigh
and by god I wanted you
to smile, to sigh out a small yes
between your legs.

[It must have been a Saturday]

because the parking lot was full
of mothers and small dogs
popping out of grocery bags.
In this one we held hands
without speaking all the way
around the store until one of us
mentioned making love
in front of the security camera.
We talked like we wanted kids,
but one of us saw something that day.
I can't remember who, or just what.

Human Aviary

Instead of burying the shoebox,
we take off our shirts and kiss
the ground. Again, the moths fly
out, the gross wonder. We're still young.
Shaped by summer and its lesions.
We toe the line between field
and sun until it's light
in our mouths.

∞

I've picked up carving linnets in the attic
of an abandoned house to hold on to
something flightless. To be uncrushing.
Outside, the wind curls talons
from the ice near what used to be
a kitchen window. If you close your eyes
you can smell the river from here.

∞

I remember us buying peppermints
from the gas station outside Florence.
Your tongue a radioactive stripe
until we drove to the ocean
where there was nothing left.

∞

Imagine this is still the late nineties.
The man scratched in rags on the bench
behind the church drinking the ship
right out of the bottle. On his back
he finally hears the angels' light
breathing. They say nothing, which is:
I've been waiting for you my whole life.

[I am dreaming in this one. You wax]

your nails mauve with streaks of teal.
I make a joke about salt water taffy,
anything to keep the polish in the air.
Your toes bend all macaroni-like
over the coffee table. You flip
the channel. It's the most normal
day in existence. Wake up. I can't.

[Two men are playing chess in a park]

in this one. Give me a shotgun to point
at my foot. I am trying to not say *remember*
anymore. But remember when we drank
warm wine in the hotel and I taught you
how to move the knight? This is like that.
Two spaces north, one space over
the apartment we used to have a name for.

Autobiographies

I am a traveling mirage. A dream circus unraveling. Because I am losing face I see your face tattooed on every neck of sky. I tell myself things like I am mayor of this garden in Idaho. Tuesdays are my Sabbath. Two juncos are playing piccolo on the shoulder of a sycamore and I am working the trunk with my silver shovel. Some jewels are edible, others bow low. I am your hickey-suck and charm necklace. Tell me I'm agreeable. Remind me why I wear a cape around the yard, a crown of light bulbs to sleep. Together we renamed ourselves Oleander. I am of York. My blanket becomes a kilt at Christmas. These are sentences within sentences within porcelain dolls. I hug them each, uncupping language with a black tongue. Sorrow and sweetness giving birth back and forth. I am growing permanent. I call out things in the long hallway of your ear as if it were still a doorway I'm allowed to enter. I've given up wearing shoes. I discuss your old underwear with myself. One of us is missing out. Here is my talismanic mania. Here is my yarn corpse. The first words ever spoken were in dinosaur. The last. I am gnawing on branches. I am not your idiot. I am. Amen.

X

I wear your pendant
around my neck
like cattle rope.

Though you're gone
still I take
for the barn.

[*I've been carving my mug shot*]

along the back of my hand for half
an hour, wondering which of me
will talk first. I want you to say
there are dreams worthy
of this growth of being
alone. This gondola for one
and I'm obsessed over what I do
and do not know. The night as hard
as drugs, the animal breathing snow,
breaking down slowly in the blackening
cold. In this one I actually want to feel
a shiver of lightning run up the sky,
my legs. What possesses the wind
to still swim through town? The church
to break out its bell and sound something
similar but not equal to absolution?
Remind me what I've become —
a pair of boots left in the garage,
taking on the old and dying
smell of everything around them.
A bird under a tire, the song
spilt from its throat with blood.

Backyard Mirage Therapy

My empty is half glass. Pots boil and boil so I water the lawn
with gasoline. Naked the only way to describe these emotional
blackouts. A tree collects kites, birds with songs too tired.
Watch them figure it out, I say aloud to no one. My headspace
is crawlspace, my knees deep down in soil. I say I could hit the
sky with a floorboard. I spit out ants. A little word fungus, a
little lung cancer in how I decide to stop talking to the moon.
I'm balding with it and the neighbor girl is playing heart & soul
on the recorder. October always just a few months away. I dig
through the garage: old tricycles and wooden tennis rackets. I
smile through a hazmat mask, tell the VHS tapes I will take
them to their leader. The car's rumbling with a handkerchief in
the muffler. The air is sweeter on this planet. Keep up, I say.
Let's soar into 44th. The windshield a lake with smoke in its
hair. Sun in the splintered corner of the rearview mirror. Let's
close our eyes. Let's try to think like an outpatient.

[That last month when we broke out]

the Ouija board, you lit votives
on my chest as if it were a river,
as if the sound of wax hardening
could reinterpret my flesh.
At night I often sit in the corner
of our old bedroom, legs in my arms,
imagining a colony of ants
streaming down my face.
I tell myself I am a dormant hive
waiting to be shaken. I let them
crawl. *The smart wasp waits and waits
and watches.* This one tends to repeat
itself: first I address the darkness
by speaking with my hands. Then
I ask it to rise (I rise), not knowing
how visible we can be without eyes.

[I went on a date with a man]

last week. He said my hands
were kaleidoscopic butterflies
and if I broke them apart
someone in India might shiver.
Said the moon's horoscope
was a deflated basketball
so I laughed. I don't love
men the way I might or ought
to these days, but you're dying
in my mind and nowhere near me
do monarchs mimic viceroys.
Or vice versa. Butterflies come
in quick stitches and knives
and public speeches. If only
each version could strip itself
of paint. If only your face were
a lottery ticket I could scratch off
with a penny. I've been dreaming
of you since February and here
it is always February. No one
believes in calendars or advent
birds. Months are actually
just the paper legs of insects,
the small wings we used to rub
into disintegration so that everything
we touched would also forget
what it feels like to fly. To know

nothing but air, lung, and song
until the song is a line of static.

Elegiac

A cancerous goat walking around
in fencepost circles is one way
to describe this. You are dead.
Everyone you loved is dead
to you and a field of charred wheat
flaking off the low Montana plains
isn't enough to say we all beg
for winter water. We contain
multitudes. Miracles still fit
into our pockets like watches,
waltzes we've not yet stepped to.
This is hardly the earth. This is
my breath unraveling. My teeth.
A way to feel dread as if you could
teach me how to reinterpret new situations
again. Tell me the sky is a blue demon
filled with elevator music. I call thunder
down the corridor of a microphone.
I want you to know in some dreams
I completely stop dreaming but I don't
wake up. Call it vacuum suck. An emotion.

River Rat

Lately I go back there alone.
Chilled kiss of a shirtless night,
jeans rolled to wading height,
cool of the current on my calves.
Water has a strange way of always
sounding like a crying woman.
I will probably drink it, pumped
and distilled, months from now
after a good workout, out
of a bottle. We are younger
than we will ever be again,
a truth as dark as my hand
in this river, which touches me
back. After the shower the stars
stop talking, forget I am even here.
Forget why I came in the first place.

[I've stopped believing in death]

and traffic lights. Some nights
I place an animal, stuffed,
on the passenger seat and drive
through town with the windows
down. I turn up the radio
and ask the weather to cry
us out. In this one all the crows
caked to the pavement still beat.
In this one every dead deer
remembers what it was like
to feed off the sweet low vines
of cherry trees. I make a bed
with wine in the laid-out trunk
and tell the invisible driver
to push into fifth and scream
the tires out of transmission.
In this one I'm the animal,
the passenger seat, the bottle
of liquid gods drinking itself
dry. The moon sticks to the sky
like a firefly. The stars shred
into goose down. I swear everything
twitches if you tell it long enough
it doesn't exist and can't ever.

[This the one holding a mug over]

the other ones like a goddamn match
being licked out by cupped darkness.
It's all I can do to not be wild. Turns out
our friends were mostly your friends.
I pinch the useless skin between
my eyes, waiting for the pressure
to say something. It never does.
I talk out loud to the mirror. Press
my cheek to it. I am hideous,
miraculous. I misquote Oscar Wilde.
Experience is merely the name men give
to their mistakes. I won't name you.

Longest Division

Say apple, blood red, and I hear
the arrow flay the opaque air.

Hear things split
in two, hairlined, molecules
flaking into atoms.

But I cannot fathom the distance
between here and her and he.

I cannot actually touch my heart.

If we walked to the grocery store
for six years, if we palmed
produce for minutes,
if we bit.

The moment the sparrow lifts
and I am still
watching the branch.

III.

HELL FEELINGS

Hypnosis

We close our eyes to arrive in the middle of a field.
A field with holes rifled through aluminum cans
and dogs whose eyes have been mistaken
for cans. We grow up all over again:
the road's gravel in our skin, the drunk sunset
drilling crimson holes down the sky's open throat.
In the distance a coal train crawls across these hills
like a glinting necklace. Grass makes sauce
of last fall's pumpkins and a horse falls to its knees
before the changing season. When we open our eyes
we will surely die, mountains only as large as our thumbs
will allow. We cannot say anything. We are so immense.

Buffalo Jump

I recall the story of an old people
who would force a stampede of buffalo
off a cliff. They would eat the raw heart
of the first to fall. Wear its tongue
like a rope around their waists.
I am trying to understand the body
as prize in new and ceremonious ways.
When we finish making love, I tell myself
it's possible to understand pleasure only
with my mind. To stop feeling the crude
oil of my joints, the lamp lit with hers.
What if we are able to hold wild geraniums
in our teeth and never speak? Grass
as a method of madness and nothing
more. I consider the slow breath
of the lone bull hovering like glass
over the ledge, watching the weight
of his family become the late night fire
dance of animal paint and canvas rhythm.
I feel my pulse twitch in my throat and begin
to dream my eyes back into the attic
of my head. This is a marbled lightning
we contain by being silent. I want the world
to know we will be as loud as the salmon
who swim upstream into their skin.

We will apologize for everything
with our chests in the wind. We will
cannibalize our names until the letters
drip garnet. Blood kettle, bright seed.

Whale Song

The stars poke through like axe
wounds, as if someone above them
lost a daughter. My God.

Bad Summon

Somewhere you are being hooded with flowers
or scattered among the glassless
Pacific. Somewhere a bone-soft boy holds a green bottle
which holds the ship of your language.
I want to tattoo your imagination onto my lungs.
Breathe out your silver hair on the cooling train car window.
What else do we have. Everyone
I don't know but love died this week and no one
can steal away their madness.
You broke cherries in your mouth and the stems
came out as failed hydrangeas. I love
you. I hate. Because the sun is a fleshed tangerine
I can't say anything is worth extreme
feelings. Please, come back
as a milk can, a hummingbird's limp
wing. Come back as the knife slipping between feather
and the cool river the muscles make.
I want to be your stepchild, the feeble knee of the ant
pushing your body closer
to the edge of water, that blood-soaked
laughter, a bread crumb worthy of wine and sucking
until all that's left is the cheek,
the bone, fucked memory. How we all become
the shape our bodies leave behind.

The Smoke Detector
Where Your Heart Should Be

Test weekly, or: how to start small fires
in the kitchen. I place my lips to your chest
where the beating is red. You throb and throb.
Read: do not paint. Read: I am learning
to understand this language of *never again*.
I take paperclips and link them like train cars,
drape them around your neck and together
we see how everything is important, or: see
owner's manual for complete instructions, or:
we take our clothes off in the dark and feel
for the walls of our bodies. Our breathing
patterns like whales signaling to each other
beneath the world. This air its own form
of water. I touch your eyes and think
luminal static, glassed lightning.

Temp/oral

If the uvula is actually a wishbone
for the throat, go ahead, break
your heart on mine. Your whale
dreams. The pot of nail soup
thawing in the garage has nothing
in common with the dartboard
of ducks hushing beneath the town
pond. Everything has its own way
of breathing and then not breathing.
You are exactly one cosmos. I open
your mouth with my finger in search
of harmony, undiscovered asteroids.
In other words what opens like a cave
has no room for birds, just a chandelier
of ice melting into what it won't become.

Axis

I want dark marble over everything I want
no longer living. Small animal outline
on the sidewalk. Above, a large bird colors in
the shape with hunger. My mouth too holds
headstones. Write your name on my teeth
and watch as your body overflows with grass.
This isn't about reasons. We have nothing to do
with grief. If we die only once let it be with fireworks
in our hair. Some nights I shake a magic eight ball
in my palms, rotating this small earth, eyes closed,
chanting *not today*. This a way of talking out loud
to no one. Of mastering death before it finds me.
I wear a pendant around the cool of my chest
and think *thunder, slab*. I get this close to vulgar.

My Friends

I want to pick them up like voodoo dolls
with stitched mouths so they can't talk
back. I tell them: do what you are going to do
to each other. Don't stop. I float a needle
down the cloth of their spines, over their eyes.
In the dark they are no longer the shapes
they were. Their hands hover like metal
detectors across each other's bodies,
closing in on the pleasures of no return.
I tell them: press hard. Breathe in.
And I know at night, in that quiet blast,
they can hear me. They turn up the music
of my bidding. Becoming, at last, terrible.
Lately I've been dreaming of burning
houses. Whole towns draped in flame.

Eventualities

I've been running a thumb
over my gums all week, tonguing

sugar, curious but not yet
ready to give in to wonder.

Jack bought a sack of powder
and I've never smoked the Christ

out of crystal. It's true,
my zodiac is a razor-fish

and tonight I'm going to shoot
for blue. What happened happens

forever. The bowling ball blow,
nitrous ecstasy. Anything with a hose

that isn't green. Down the street
a pair of shoes dangle like wet

laundry from telephone wire.
A kid without teeth

runs through the bushes,
pretending his hands are fire

trucks. His mother's eyes
turn to glass each afternoon,

two moons slow to orbit,
and I know when she reaches

for the mail she often forgets
who he is. Don't we all.

What Dying Was Like

They carried my body like a horse rug
through the backyard. All skin, no air.
Potted peas hanging from rope, a wood
pecker siphoning years from the heartbeat
of a willow. I was looking up from the black
hollow of my shadow like a sea cow following
the shoreline. So in love with the diesel
greasing the grass blades, the light finger
print of each tip on my accordioned back.
The march was short, like a dream
in which hours occur in drams. I took
this time to remember the musical measures
of old lovers' neck stones. The different
ways the sun would soprano through
their hair. And I remembered the glass
face of hate. How it was sharp from start
to finish. And I wondered the number
of who still felt it now. I pictured them
hearing the news that so-and-so
from the college years or that desk job
finally absorbed the earth like a sponge —
that alchemical mixture of emotion, of nothing
to say but sure, sorry, send over the details.
I focused on my mother and her fingernails,
always inked with soil, tomato blood, keeping
my father from losing himself to God.
My older brother weeping into the bed sheets

and his older brother ignoring the phone call.
I looked up to the salmon sun over Montana
rivers, shouldered by mountains, atheistic
to the satellites blinking out Morse. I recalled
a girl choking on the lightness of morphine.
How her blonde braids were donated
to the homeless. Some beads of rain never
blossom into energy. This sadness and evidence
must be specific. We look down at our chests
to find not a knife, but a sparkler, just lit.

Growing Down

We buy animals to replace other
animals. We fold paper and give wings
to a swan. This isn't the way we imagined
our dying — rolling around in the clay
to better understand fire. Cracking
a little like sunburst in the middle.
Quietly we scream into the earth,
quietly we give back. We're learning
what it means to say yes. To sink
beneath the soil until a girl walks by
scattering seeds, placing the watering can
gently on our heads. The idea of moisture
so close we can taste the metal. So thin
it begins to melt, then dissolve.

Smoke Tones

I.

Something about this town is old rubber.
If it isn't dangling from the bed
of a red truck, a deer is
gnawing flowers from my palm.
Everyone here drinks alone
together. The stars are bulbs
of Jurassic insects, paused lightning.
They curse down our open shirts.
I wet my fingers and try to pinch one
like a wick, forgetting how distance closes
in on us from past and future centuries.
This night is a brown, miniature train:
we widen our mouths into tunnels.

II.

Some nights are thick as milk.
What we abandon retracts
with small clouds on its back.
We fight the urge to torment
bottles into the ground,
but we are weak. Danger
speaks from within. Distills
the shape our bodies make
the way some roses swallow
gold until everything is whole
and a bee sings out.

III.
Everyone here pretends to be grass,
wind-licked, though we are only
kidding ourselves. The girls want us
to drink another one for them
even after they've gone to bed
in some strange guy's average arms.
So we do two, twelve, trouble
we've sunk into before and before
that and after. After, always.

IV.
There are more fields than we have fingers
to run them through. We pour beer
into the creek and press our ears
to the earth where the rocks shift,
move water south toward our lips.
We are conch shells, stethoscopes,
children in the grove saying
no more, never evermore.
We will not go home.

Another Language

Someone once told me
if I could dream it I should
drink it. So I let the word boil
like black, unlit oil in my throat,
waiting for anyone to strike
a match. Tell me you could
hate me. Tell me and I will turn
into a bouquet of white and blue
flames. Last week in Montana
a woman took a cattle brand
to her stomach. The small,
not-quite body inside her body
pinched out by the red fingers
of hot metal. I have an addiction
to stories like this. I cannot sleep
anymore. My eyes light up
like aquarium fish in the night.
Give me the farmer who slow-bleeds
his pigs, the old professor who cuts
harmonica slits into his wrists.
Let me feed off. Let me hate
and be hated. There are
immeasurable qualities
in the dark. A face without
a hand to trace it. The voice
taken from the mouth, saying
come with me and don't look back.

My America

These days those days become. We go back
to dipping arrows deep into the blue necks
of dart frogs to siphon out our enemies
from the earth. Back to stretching back
the bow like a wooden moon until our hands
bleed lost centuries. We cannot stop at grief.
We set the sky on fire and watch as halogen
doves lift like bone ash from the flesh lights.
If we know death it is only from the eyes
of children running endlessly into lakes.
We become a new breed of murder. Translate:
on the sidewalks, halved faces. On the stars
our names erasing. This flag every shade of vein,
scorched vine. Each window bead of rain a *tap tap*
gunmetal. A way to shatter with teeth in our hair.
These days we hold a magnifying glass to the sun
and wait until our faces melt into murals. Time
only heals the wounds of the buried. Time draws
water from the well and downs it whole. What if
we are gods or devils, mythic creatures screaming
amnesia from the hull of the ship. What if
we never closed our eyes. There will be a day
when the oceans fill with bodies. When floating
becomes a measurement, a dram, a quiet noun.

Touching Down

So much for
the lone cannon

up to its ears
in winter wheat

in the Kansas
of someone's dying

backyard. So much
for the choke

cherries sprouting
out its mouth.

Here, the dead
stay dead.

What's left is
still covered

in marrow reds.
Bags for the bags

of bodies. Shovels
more familiar

with grief
than gardens.

So much for
the anthem

loosening
in the throats

of porch cats,
yellow eyes

floating like
fireflies, sliced

moons over fields
siphoning bones

from the earth
as if there were

a milk in this world
sweet enough to last.

Notes and Acknowledgments

Loads of gratitude to my family for all their support over the years, especially my wife Natalie for moving to Missoula with me toward this new life and the home we've now made. And to my brother Justin for sharing the same mind but with a better heart. Thanks to my closest readers for endless nights & insights & whiskey edits: Jeff Whitney (my poetry pope), Caylin Capra-Thomas, Elliott Niblock, BJ Soloy, Jenny Montgomery, & Bradley Harrison. Thanks to my mentors Joanna Klink, Jamie D'Agostino, Ed Skoog, Prageeta Sharma, Chris Dombrowski, Joe Benevento, Elizabeth Robinson, and all those at the University of Montana. None of these poems would exist without you and your guidance.

Special thanks to editors Sean Shearer, Diane Goettel, and Kelly Forsythe for first publishing many of these poems in larger chapbook manuscript chunks. And to Ryan & Jenny Montgomery for supporting this book and my writing in ways too numerous to mention.

Like a good cliché, I am grateful to the mountains & rivers & night skies of Montana for reminding me of the connection between power and death, belonging and isolation.

The title poem "Bad Summon" is an elegy for CD Wright, and won the 2016 *Meridian* Editor's Prize in poetry.

The poem "The Smoke Detector Where Your Heart Should Be" was inspired by The Magnetic Fields' song "The Cactus Where Your Heart Should Be."

The line "Experience is merely the name men give / to their mistakes" is an actual quote from Oscar Wilde, not a misquote as mentioned in the poem "[This the one holding a mug over]".

Grateful acknowledgment is given to the editors of the following publications, in which some of these poems first appeared, sometimes in other forms:

Adroit – "Human Aviary" / "Buffalo Jump"

BOAAT – "The New World" / "[I've stopped believing in death]"

The Boiler – "Hypnosis" / "Eventualities" / "Another Language"

Chariton Review – "River Rat"

Connotation Press: A Poetry Congeries – "[Two men are playing chess in a park]" / "[I've been carving my mug shot]" / "[That last month when we broke out]" / "[I am dreaming in this one. You wax]" / "[I went on a date with a man]"

Cream City Review – "X"

DIAGRAM – "Touching Down"

Forklift, Ohio – "My Friends" / "Once"

Great American Literary Magazine – "Earthenware"

Guernica – "Suture"

H_NGM_N – "[Yesterday I found myself awake]" / "[In this one we aren't exactly drowning]" / "[In this one you haven't left]" / "[A swarm of neighborhood dogs]" / "[In this one you are taking the creek]" / "[This the one holding a mug over]"

Kenyon Review – "The Unaccounted"

Meridian – "Bad Summon" / "I'm Keeping the Wooden Horse"

Muzzle – "Smoke Screen"

Nashville Review – "What Dying Was Like"

NightBlock – "After You Left"

NOON – "Whale Song"

Pacifica – "Evening News"

Prelude – "Barbiturate Talismania" / "Axis"

RHINO – "Longest Division"

Salt Hill – "My America"

Sonora Review – "Translating Poorly"

Spork – "Sisyphus Self" / "Discipline" / "Tem/poral" / "Elegiac" / "[In this one I'm wearing a paper bag]"

Spry – "Minor Dogma"

Tinderbox – "Autobiographies" / "Overdose"

Toad – "Smoke Tones"

Vinyl Poetry – "The Smoke Detector Where Your Heart Should Be" / "Practicing Invisible" / "Growing Down"

Whiskey Island – "Walk Slowly, Don't Stare"

** Portions of this manuscript have appeared in the chapbooks *Smoke Tones (Phantom Books, 2015)* and *Radio Silence (Black Lawrence Press, 2016)*.

*** The section *[HIDEOUS] MIRACULOUS* was published as a chapbook by *BOAAT Press* (2015).

PREVIOUS WINNERS OF THE AGHA SHAHID ALI PRIZE IN POETRY

Ann Lauinger
Persuasions of Fall

Jacqueline Berger
Things That Burn

Bino A. Realuyo
*The Gods We Worship
Live Next Door*

Jane Springer
Dear Blackbird,

Susan McCabe
Descartes' Nightmare

Jessica Garratt
Fire Pond

Jon Wilkins
Transistor Rodeo

Jennifer Perrine
In the Human Zoo

Kim Young
Night Radio

Mark Jay Brewin Jr.
Scrap Iron

Kara Candito
Spectator

Sara Wallace
The Rival

Davis McCombs
lore